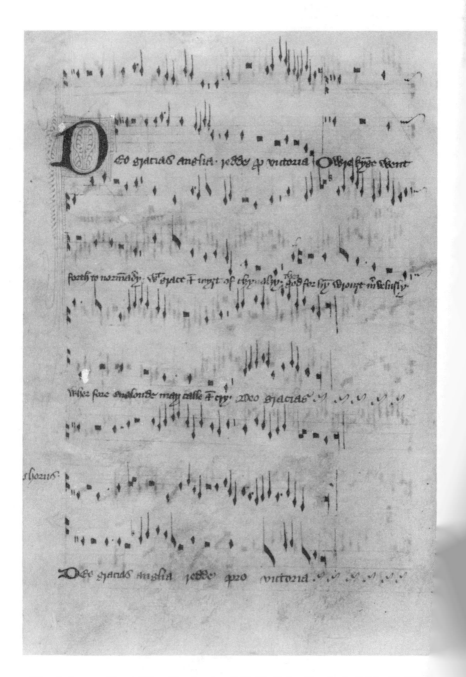

The Agincourt Carol ("Deo Gracias Anglia") (Bodleian Ms. Arch. Selden B. 26). By permission of the Bodleian Library, Oxford.

An English Medieval and Renaissance Song Book

Part Songs and Sacred Music
for One to Six Voices

Edited by
NOAH GREENBERG

With an Introduction by
JOEL NEWMAN

DOVER PUBLICATIONS, INC.
Mineola, New York

Bibliographical Note

This Dover edition, first published in 2000, is a republication of *An English Songbook: Part songs and Sacred music of the Middle Ages and Renaissance for one to six voices / Edited by Noah Greenberg, with an Introduction by Joel Newman*, originally published by Doubleday & Company, Inc., Garden City, 1961.

The book is complete and unabridged except for the omission of decorative (non-musical) illustrations scattered throughout the original edition, and a slight reordering of its prefatory pages.

International Standard Book Number: 0-486-41374-8

Manufactured in the United States of America
Dover Publications, Inc., 31 East 2nd Street, Mineola, N.Y. 11501

ACKNOWLEDGMENTS

Acknowledgment is hereby gratefully made to the following publishers and copyright holders for permission to reprint the selections listed below:

The American Institute of Musicology for "Alleluia psallat" from *Worcester Fragments*, published by the American Institute of Musicology, by permission of Dr. Armen Carapetyan.

Appleton-Century-Crofts, Inc., for "Angelus ad Virginem" from *Examples of Music before 1400*, edited by Harold Gleason. Copyright 1942 by F. S. Crofts & Co., Inc.

The Carnegie United Kingdom Trust for the "Gloria" from "Westron Wynde Mass," "O Lord, increase my faith," "Agnus Dei," "Salvator mundi," "Nunc dimittis," and "Emendemus in melius" from *Tudor Church Music*, published by the Oxford University Press.

The Clarendon Press, Oxford, for "Worldes blis ne last," "Edi Beo," "Jesu Cristes milde moder" from *English Lyrics of the Thirteenth Century*, ed. Carleton Brown.

Galaxy Music Corporation for "Deo Gracias Anglia," "Nowel sing we bothe al and some," and "Nova, Nova" from *Musica Britannica*, Vol. IV—*Mediaeval Carols*, copyright 1958 by The Royal Musical Association, printed by permission of The Royal Musical Association and Stainer and Bell, Ltd.

Music and Letters for "Edi beo" from Vol. XVI (1935) transcribed by Manfred Bukofzer.

The Musical Quarterly for "Alas departynge is ground of woo" from *The Musical Quarterly* for January 1942. Copyright 1942 by G. Schirmer, Inc.

W. W. Norton & Company, Inc., for "Jesu Cristes milde moder," "Beata progenies," "Crist and Sainte Marie," and "Man mei longe" from *Music in the Middle Ages*, by Gustave Reese.

The Plainsong and Mediaeval Music Society for "Sanctus" by Roy Henry from *The Old Hall Manuscript*, Vol. III.

University of California Press for "Sumer Is Icumen In" from *Sumer Is Icumen In: A Revision*, by Manfred Bukofzer.

TO TONI

EDITOR'S NOTE

I would like to thank Joel Newman for a considerable share in making this book; he was particularly useful in locating materials and in editorial tasks. May I also thank Walter R. Davis of the Massachusetts Institute of Technology, Dr. Jean Misrahi of Fordham, and Dr. David Goldstein for their helpful assistance.

I am grateful to the following libraries for the use of source material from their collections: The British Museum for the Henry VIII, Cornysh, and Pygott works in Add. Ms. 31922 and for original editions of Morley, Wilbye, and Weelkes; The Folger Shakespeare Library, Washington, D. C., for Byrd's *Songs of Sundrie Natures.*

Noah Greenberg

CONTENTS

11

INTRODUCTION

Reader, this is not just one more songbook to open on your piano. Rather select your best table, one without sharp edges, and load it down with good cheer, leaving place for this book. Then gather around your forces, partake, and take part. Or, since the collection begins with some lyrics from the old "monophonic" days when music and melody were one and the same, try these pieces alone after your morning coffee. Perhaps, like Sir Toby, you and your companions may want to roar out Cornysh's *Blow Thy Horne Hunter* and Ravenscroft's *New Oysters* in some wine cellar or on a country lane with a rushing wind to play hob with the parts. Muster as many melodic instruments as you can find—every rebec, viol, gittern, and lute you know of. But failing these, recorders, violins, flutes, cellos, and the like will make do splendidly. Use them to fill in for absent singing friends, or to reinforce your voices, or even, in time of chills and laryngitis, to play a piece from top to bottom as a purely instrumental project. But use the piano, the guitar, or the harpsichord only *in extremis;* these will do best if they pretend to be melodic instruments, lining out a voice part or two. Perhaps, after all, the piano can best serve as a convenient music rack.

Convivial and hearty music is here in plenty, but side by side with it is reflective, elegiac, and ritual utterance — which prompts a quick modulation to serious commentary. When as many as forty-seven compositions from so large a span of time are assembled, it may be profitable to take an overview, grouping them according to function. Nine of the works are liturgical in use, music for the service. Three belong to the Ordinary of the Roman Catholic Mass: a *Sanctus* by Henry IV, part of the *Gloria* from Taverner's *Westron Wynde* Mass, and the *Agnus Dei* from a beautiful four-part Mass by Tallis. Shorter settings of texts from the Proper or the Office, called by the all-inclusive term motets, include an *Alleluia* from Worcester, Power's sonorous *Beata progenies,* Dunstable's *Sancta Maria,* and two Elizabethan examples, the *Salvator Mundi* by Tallis for use at Compline on Christmas and Byrd's Ash Wednesday motet, *Emendemus in Melius.* After the Reformation, Mass and Office were replaced by Services and the motet gave way to the anthem. Gibbons' *O Lord, Increase My Faith* illustrates the generally simpler texture of the anthem. The *Nunc Dimittis* (Simeon's Canticle) from Tomkins' First Evensong Service exemplifies the sumptuous style of Anglican cathedral music which often demanded soloists, full choir, and instrumental support from organ and viols.

England's long-standing tradition of popular religious lyric poetry is represented by the earliest moralizing and religious songs (Nos. 1–5), by the justly famous fifteenth-century carols (Nos. 13–15), and by such part songs of piety as Byrd's *Susanna Fayre* and Ravenscroft's *O Lord, Turn Not Away* and *Remember Oh Thou Man.*

Secular compositions often fall into two classes, sophisticated works for courtly or skilled domestic music-making and "popular," middle-class music. The high-art genre is well represented here by the poignant *Alas Departynge,* the part songs of Henry VIII's circle (Nos. 16–20), and a large group of Elizabethan madrigals, canzonets, and ayres (Nos. 24, 26–38). Good sources of popular Elizabethan part song are the Ravenscroft collections, *Pammelia, Deuteromelia,* and *Mellismata,* whose great appeal is evident from their frequent reprintings. Such lusty catches and songs are the best advertisement for the "Merrie England" aspect of Elizabethan and Jacobean life.

If the reader is willing, another quick ramble through the collection is now proposed, this time considering the music from the point of view of its style, the sum of all its "personality" traits. The early twelfth- and thirteenth-century songs represent monophony, the purest melody unencumbered by harmony. Until the ninth and tenth centuries this had been the normal manner of music all over the world. When the author of *Sir Orfeo* (c. 1300) pictured the dinner music provided by " . . . trompours and tabourers, Harpours fele, and crouders. Miche melody thay maked all . . . " he stressed this element of melody, the foundation for such great treasuries of medieval music as Gregorian chant, the songs of the Provençal *trobador* and the French *trouvère,* the Spanish *Cantigas,* and the Italian *Laude.*

Though the annals of early polyphony (the new art of combined melody) ring with names like Chartres, St. Martial in Limoges, and Paris, England was soon to take a hand in the game, and according to her own rules at that. During the years of French Gothic hegemony, music was dominated by the "perfect" intervals, the octave, fifth, and fourth, producing austere and hollow (though by no means unpleasant) sounds. Theory ruled these intervals perfect, and practice followed theory, since medieval man customarily trusted any authority save his own senses. The English, however, seemed to prefer the more suave third and sixth, in spite of the fact that theoretical tomes decreed these intervals "imperfect." Our seven pieces of early polyphony (Nos. 5–11), are very different one from another but share in common a characteristic English love of full sound and of harmony based on the third: the melodious duo, *Edi Beo;* the beloved, bouncing Sumer canon, an outstanding musical achievement, though scholars argue over its date of birth; the Worcester *Alleluya Psallat,* surely the most cheerful *Alleluia* on record and one of the most grateful medieval compositions; the sacred pieces by Power and Roy Henry from the *Old Hall* manuscript.

Early fifteenth-century music, whose sweetly "pan-consonant" sound was now established in both English and continental styles, is illustrated here by a motet of the first English composer, John Dunstable and by some lively carols, one of which celebrates Henry V's victory at Agincourt in 1415.

Secular music burgeoned from the musically fertile sixteenth century, a good deal of it issuing from courtly centers where music and letters were cultivated. Such a group of poets and musicians surrounded Henry VIII. We find an index of their activities in a beautifully written manuscript which is the source for Nos. 17–20, part songs by the King himself and by William Cornysh. Modeled on French courtly *chansons,* these songs are polyphonic, though simply so. A radically different style distinguishes the church music of Henry's generation. In the works of masters like Taverner and Tallis, the traditional penchant for full sonority and for mildly acid chromatic clashings, especially at cadences, is joined to elements from Flemish Renaissance style — high-arching and winding melodic lines and complicated part weaving. Tallis and Byrd sum up this synthesis in England's last great Catholic music.

If Queen Elizabeth's time witnessed the disastrous failure of the Spanish Armada, it also saw a decisive victory of High Renaissance Italian culture over England. In music, forms like the madrigal and its lighter brethren, the *canzonetta* and *balletto,* were welcomed, translated, and ultimately transformed. Byrd, who wrote the first English madrigals "after the Italian vaine," betrays some uneasy national pride by rejecting the Italianate term, preferring to call his madrigalian publications *Songes.* Morley, on the other hand, accepted the Italian bounty wholeheartedly. After a study of his models, in the course of which he published two books of Italian madrigals with translated texts, he effected a fusion of both serious and light foreign types with native English spirit. The resulting English madrigal was no mean achievement. Its vitality and freshness is especially striking when we consider that its model, which had begun life some fifty years earlier, was now rather overripe and tired. The Italian composers most favored were Croce and Marenzio. Gesualdo's supercharged manneristic experiments were also appreciated, some of his harmonic findings being used to good effect by Dowland, Wilbye, and Weelkes, the serious madrigalists. Morley, though so eminently associated with the light touch, could also turn out as grave and poignant a madrigal as the rest (see Nos. 28 and 29).

A specifically English contribution to the madrigal family was the ayre. This could be performed in two ways — as a part song (Nos. 31–32) or as a solo song to the lute (see *An Elizabethan Song Book* for a collection of lute ayres). Many of the madrigalists published volumes of ayres, although the genre seems to have encouraged composers like John Dowland, the poet-musician Thomas Campion, and Robert Jones to devote themselves almost exclusively to it.

After Elizabeth's death in 1603, moods of pessimism and doubt presaged in art works produced during her reign emerged so clearly that scholars speak of the "Jacobean melancholy." This new intensity of feeling blended very well with a similar trend imported from Italy — the "New Music" developed in Florence and Mantua. Here the emphasis was placed on solo song, performed so as to wring the utmost in affective expression from intense and sensual verse. The impact of the new style was not immediately felt in the sphere of the polyphonic song, but rather in masque music and the ayres by such composers as Alfonso Ferrabosco, Jr., John Coprario, John Daniel, and Dowland. At least one master, Tomkins, ignored these trends entirely, and continued to compose in the vein of Byrd, his teacher, well into the Caroline age.

Once there was a brand of Victorian madness which claimed that English-men were unmusical. A glance at this volume should kill off any lingering symptoms of that disease; for England was once a true nest of singing birds. Eminent foreigners sounded the praises of her musical achievements unhesitatingly. But certain modern apologists have overstated the case in the propagandistic spirit of the opening of Morley's theoretical book, *Plaine and Easie Introduction to Practicall Musicke* where hapless Philomathes tells of his shame when, after being requested to sing madrigals with the other guests after dinner, he had to admit that he could not and, in his words, "every one began to wonder; yea, some whispered to others demanding how I was brought up, so that upon shame of mine ignorance I go now to seek out mine old friend Master Gnorimus [Morley himself], to make myself his scholar." Nowadays we interpret such documents with caution. We do not believe that every Elizabethan courtier could read off a madrigal part at sight. But we do believe that a substantial number of intelligentsia in the Renaissance could function musically. And those others, unlike today's crop of passive music lovers, knew at least that they ought to be able to take part, because their courtiers' handbooks told them so! The Tudors alone furnish an exemplary instance. Is there a ruler alive today who could live up to a Venetian ambassador's description of Henry VIII as ". . . very accomplished; a good musician; composes well; is a most capital horseman; a fine jouster; speakes good French, Latin and Spanish . . ."? Another Venetian envoy reported that Queen Mary "takes great pleasure in playing on the lute and spinet, and is a very good performer on both instruments; and indeed before her accession she taught many of her maids of honour . . . " There seems no need to cite any of the documents vouching for Elizabeth's proficiency.

In short, a very healthy amateur tradition obtained. It was by no means limited to royalty, although compositions by a Lancaster and a Tudor take well-merited places in these pages. The most interesting thing is that this tradition coexisted with the other tradition of mastery and virtuosity. The master's nimbleness did not at that time disenchant the bumbling amateur, though a regrettable schism was to grow increasingly pronounced, beginning in the baroque age. In our own time it is the amateur who furnishes the enthusiastic audience for music from before 1750; the professional musician, trained in the spirit of the romantic movement, tends to look at it askance. But "Time and love with gladnesse, Once ere long will provide for this . . . " as Morley sang, and will heal the estrangement. In the process, which goes on apace, collections such as this one, lovingly compiled by a skilled musician associated with highly professional performance standards, can provide balm.

Columbia University

Joel Newman

SOME SUGGESTED READING

Auden, W. H. "Words and Notes." Introduction to *An Elizabethan Song Book* (Doubleday, New York, 1955)

Bukofzer, Manfred. *Studies in Medieval & Renaissance Music* (Norton, New York, 1950)

"Sumer Is Icumen In," A Revision (U. of Calif., Berkeley, 1944)

Greene, Richard L. *The Early English Carols* (Oxford, 1935). Introduction

Grove's Dictionary of Music and Musicians, 5th edition (St. Martin's Press, New York, 1955). Biographical articles

Harrison, Frank L. *Music in Medieval Britain* (Routledge, London, 1958)

Mellers, Wilfrid. "Words and Music in Elizabethan England," in *The Age of Shakespeare,* ed. by Boris Ford (Penguin, London, 1956). Pp. 386–415

New Oxford History of Music
Vol. II: Early Medieval Music up to 1300 (Oxford, London, 1954)
Vol. III: Ars Nova and the Renaissance (Oxford, London, 1959)

Reese, Gustave. *Music in the Middle Ages* (Norton, New York, 1940). Chapter 14
Music in the Renaissance (Norton, New York, 1954). Chapter 15

Woodfill, Walter L. *Musicians in English Society from Elizabeth to Charles I* (Princeton, 1953)

An English Medieval and Renaissance Song Book

NOTE ON EDITORIAL POLICY

The following rules were observed by the editor in preparing this volume:

Bar lines have been added throughout, there being none in the original. These have been placed at regular metrical intervals where possible.

Dynamics and tempo indications are editorial and are intended merely as suggestions to the performer.

Note values have in most cases been reduced to one half or one quarter of the original values.

Accidentals indicated in parentheses are editorial; those appearing without parentheses before the notes are original; accidentals above the note, without parentheses, are warning signs.

Text underlay and spelling is original wherever possible and editorial underlay appears in italics.

Time signatures in brackets are editorial.

Although the pieces have been transcribed in their original keys, the performers should have no hesitation about transposing to higher or lower keys to suit the requirements of their vocal ensemble.

CRIST AND SAINTE MARIE

ST. GODRIC (*died* 1170)

Monophonic song forms an important part of the music of the Middle Ages, and its roots lie in the great plainsong literature of early times. Following the Norman Conquest, the earliest surviving English songs are those of St. Godric, a Saxon who lived a hermit's existence in Northern England during the twelfth century. His *Crist and Sainte Marie* can best be described as a miniature drama in which Godric's dead sister, surrounded by angels, tells of her journey to heaven.

e   Swa   on   sca-   mel   me   i-

led- - -   de   that   ic   on   this- *se*

er- -   de   ne   sil- - -   de   Wid

mi- ne   ba-   re   fo-   te   i- tre- di- -   e.

1st tempo
Angels again:

Ky- ri- e- ley-   son.   Chri- ste-   ley-   son.

Angels again:

Ky- ri- e- ley- son. Chri- ste e- le-   y-   son.

CRIST AND SAINTE MARIE

> Lord have mercy.
> Christ have mercy.
> Christ and St. Mary so led me on a footstool
> that I did not tread on this earth with my bare foot.
> Lord have mercy. Christ have mercy.
> Lord have mercy. Christ have mercy.

MAN MEI LONGE

ANONYMOUS (XIIIth century)

MAN MEI LONGE

The art of the troubadour and trouvère—along with its Spanish and German counterparts—survives in many continental manuscripts. Though English minstrel songs were widely sung throughout medieval Britain by the wandering poet-musicians, very little of this music remains. *Man mei longe* and *Worldes blis ne last* are two moralizing songs whose melancholy mood is in sharp contrast to the spirited English instrumental dance music of this period.

With motion

T (S&A) *mf* Man mei lon- ge him li- ves

we- - - ne,___ ac of- te him ___ ·li-

yet the wreinch; fair we- der of- te him went to

re- - - ne,⌣ an fer- li- che ____ ma-
ket is blench. *marked* Thar- vo- re, man, thu
the bi- thench, ____ al sel va- lu-
i the gre- ne, wel- a- wey! nis
King ne Que- ne that ne sel
drin- ke of deth- is drench. Man, er thu
fal- le of thi ⌐ bench, thu sin- ne a- quench.

MAN MEI LONGE

Long may man ween his life to be but oft for him there waits a trick;
fair weather often turns to rain, and sunshine is wondrously made.
Therefore, man, bethink thyself—all thy green youth shall fade. Well-
a-day! there is neither king nor queen who shall not drink the draught
of death. Man, ere thou fallest off thy bench, quench thy sin.

WORLDES BLIS NE LAST

ANONYMOUS (XIIIth century)

World-es_____ blis ne last no_____

thro- we, Hit wit ant wend a- wey a-

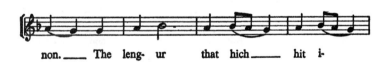

non._____ The leng- ur that hich_____ hit i-

kno- we,__ The lasse hic_____ find- e_____

27

pris ther- on. ___ For al hit ___ is i-

meynd wyd___ ka- re, Mid so- re- we ant wid___

u- vel ___ fa- re, Ant at the last- e

poue- re ant ba- re Hit let mon wen hit

gin- net a- gon. Al the blis- se, this___

he- re ant___ the- re ___ Bi- lou- keth at___

hend- e ___ wop ant ___ mon. ___

WORLDES BLIS NE LAST

The world's joy lasts no time at all, it departs and fades away at once. The longer I know it, the less value I find in it. For it is all mixed with troubles, with sorrows and misfortune, and at the last, when it begins to pass away, it leaves a man poor and naked. All the joy, both here and there, is finally encompassed by weeping and lamentation.

JESU CRISTES MILDE MODER

ANONYMOUS (XIIIth century)

The anonymous pieces *Jesu Cristes milde moder* and *Edi beo thu hevene Quene* are beautiful examples of early polyphony. They are composed in the *gymel* style—a kind of English duo writing that favors the intervals "third" and "sixth" and creates the illusion of two voices moving in parallel motion when, in actuality, they always cross each other. Both pieces date from the second half of the thirteenth century. Because of their length only the opening and closing verses of *Jesu. Cristes* and the first stanza of *Edi beo* are given.

that he was i- pi- ned on.

pp The sone heng, the mo- der stud _____

and bi- held hire child- es blud _____

wu it of hise wund- es ran.

stronger
mf Neu- e blis- se he us brou- te

that man- kin so de- re bou- te,

and for us gaf is de- re lif.

Glade and bli- the thu us ma- ke

for thi swe- te so- nes sa- ke,

e- di mai- den blis- ful wif.

Quen of e- vene for thi blis- se

lithe al hu- re so- ri- nes- se

JESU CRISTES MILDE MODER

Jesu Cristes gentle mother stood and beheld her son pinned to the cross. The son hung, the mother stood and beheld her child's blood running from his wounds. New bliss he brought, bought dearly for mankind, and he gave his dear life for us. Thou makest us glad and blithe for thy sweet son's sake, be thou blissful, virgin wife!

EDI BEO THU HEVENE QUENE

ANONYMOUS (XIVth century)

oth- er nis. On the hit___ is
wel- eth sene of al- le wim- men thu
hav- est the pris, mi swet- e
le- ye- di her mi bene and
reu___ of me___ zif thi___ wille is.

EDI BEO THU HEVENE QUENE

Happy be thou, heavenly Queen, man's comfort and angel's bliss.
Mother unstained and maiden clean, such in world none other is.
Of thee easily it is seen that of all women thou hast the prize.
My sweet lady, hear my boon and rue of me if thy will is.

SUMER IS ICUMEN IN

ANONYMOUS (XIV*th* *century*)

This is the most famous of all medieval compositions and appears here in the version by the late Manfred Bukofzer. There has been dispute among scholars about this remarkable canonic piece. It is traditionally dated from the thirteenth century, but Bukofzer has attempted to prove that it is from the early fourteenth. His transcription restores what appears to be the duple meter and *Cu-cu* call (see measure 19, highest part) of the original, apparently altered by a later scribe.

aft- er lomb, aft- er cal- ve cu; Bul- loc ster- teth
Lhouth

cu; Aw- e ble- teth. aft- er lomb, aft- er cal- ve
Lhouth

nu, Sing Cu- cu; Aw- e ble- teth

blow- eth med, And the wo- de nu, Sing Cu-
springth

cu nu, sing Cu- cu, sing Cu-

cu, sing Cu- cu nu, sing Cu-

buck- e ver- teth, Mu- rie sing Cu- cu.

cu; Bul- loc ster- teth buck- e ver- teth,

aft- er lomb, Lhouth aft- er cal- ve cu;

cu; Aw- e ble- teth aft- er lomb, Lhouth

cu nu, sing Cu- cu,

cu, sing cu- cu nu,

37

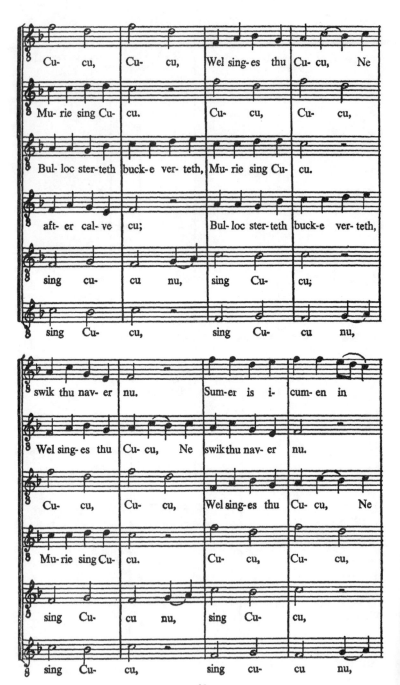

40

41

ALLELUYA PSALLAT

ANONYMOUS (*early* XIV*th century*)
This glorious *Alleluya* comes to us from a body of sacred music known to scholars as the Worcester Fragments, remnants of a great repertoire composed in the late thirteenth and early fourteenth centuries for Worcester Cathedral. Although the music shows the influence of an earlier French tradition, employing techniques more conservative than those used in the contemporary French style, one sees here the emergence of a rich English polyphonic art.

42

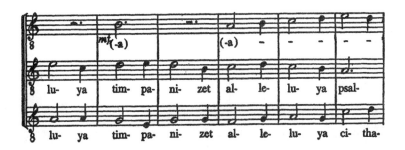

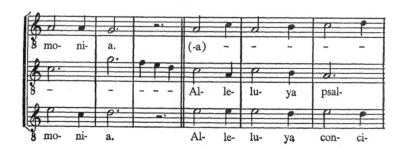

ALLELUYA PSALLAT

Alleluia sings this congregation, Alleluia, with cymbals and zithers, Alleluia, the joyous crowd in harmony sings, Alleluia, to God praise and glory. Alleluia.

ANGELUS AD VIRGINEM

ANONYMOUS (xiv*th century*)

Chaucer, describing Nicholas, the clerk, in the "Miller's Tale," writes:

> *And all above ther lay a gay sautrye,*
> *On which he made a-nightes melodye,*
> *So swetely that al the chamber rang,*
> *And Angelus ad Virginem he sang.*

This tune and polyphonic settings of it appear in the thirteenth century, and Chaucer's reference one hundred years later attests to its great popularity. In this version the melody lies in the middle voice, and the harmony is based on a progression of triads of the first inversion—a style distinctly English in origin.

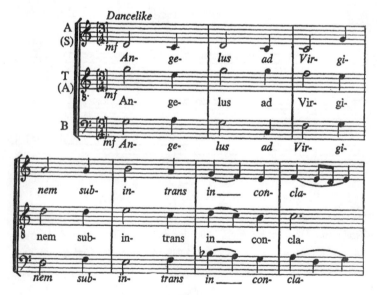

46

ANGELUS AD VIRGINEM

The Angel said to the Virgin, stealing into the chamber and calming her fearfulness: Hail, Queen of Virgins, the Lord of heaven and earth shalt thou conceive and bear in virginity, the saviour of man; thou art become the gate of heaven and redressor of wrongs.

J.N.

BEATA PROGENIES

LEONEL POWER (*died* 1445)

Leonel Power was one of the great masters of the first half of the fifteenth century, but very little is known of his life other than his possible connection with Christ Church, Canterbury. As with his more famous contemporary, Dunstable, Leonel reflects the rich cultural interchange between England and France during this period. The delicate *Beata progenies*, which appears in the Old Hall Manuscript, is written in a simple style, employing a plainsong melody in the middle voice.

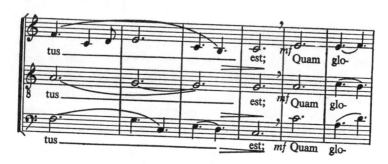

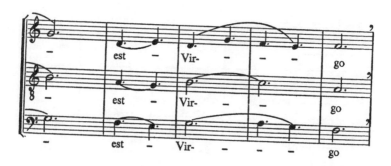

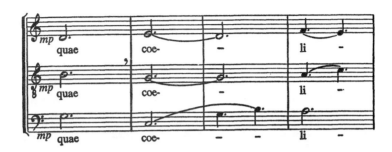

BEATA PROGENIES

Blessed progeny whence Christ was born. How glorious is the Virgin who gave birth to the King of heaven!

ALAS DEPARTYNGE IS
GROUND OF WOO

ANONYMOUS (XV*th century*)

A considerable quantity of medieval English sacred music has survived, but pitifully few examples of secular song remain. The anonymous *Alas departynge is ground of woo*—one of a number of songs with English text found in continental sources—appears in the Mellon *Chansonnier*, a collection of Burgundian origin now at Yale University. In the original the upper part is without text; it has been added here so that the piece may be performed by two singers.

Sadly—in halves

52

SANCTA MARIA

JOHN DUNSTABLE (*c.* 1370-1453)

One of the greatest composers of his time, Dunstable was musician to
the Duke of Bedford during the reigns of Henry V and VI. His music
was well known on the continent and exerted a strong influence on the
young Burgundian musicians, Dufay and Binchois. The bulk of his compositions survive in continental manuscripts rather than English ones, perhaps because of his travels in Europe. The Marian motet *Sancta Maria*
can be performed either as an alto solo with two instruments or for
voices alone.

SANCTA MARIA

Holy Mary, in this world there has arisen none like you among women.
Blooming like the rose, fragrant as the lily, pray for us, holy Mother
of God.

SANCTUS

ROY HENRY (HENRY IV [?] 1367-1413)

One of the most important sources of medieval polyphony is the Old Hall manuscript, a large collection of sacred works by English and continental composers. Two of the compositions are by a *Roy Henry*, and recent evidence seems to indicate this was Henry IV. His travels in Europe, before he ascended the throne in 1399, acquainted him with the magnificent households of Charles VI of France, the Duke of Berry, and Philip the Bold. The rich musical life of the Royal Chapels of the Lancastrian kings was indebted to such continental models.

59

san- na in_____

san- na in_____

san- na in _____

ex- cel- - - - - - -

ex- cel- - - - - - -

ex- cel- - - - - - -

flowing

- - sis. p Be- - ne- di-

- - sis. p Be- - ne- di-

- - sis. p Be- - ne- di-

- - ctus qui_____ ve-

- - ctus qui_____ ve-

- ctus qui_____ ve-

- nit____ in no- mi- ne _____

- nit in no- mi- ne _____

- nit in no- mi- ne_____

SANCTUS

Holy, Holy, Holy, Lord of hosts. Heaven and earth are full of Thy
glory. Hosanna in the highest! Blessed is he that cometh in the name
of the Lord. Hosanna in the highest!

DEO GRACIAS ANGLIA

The Agincourt Carol

ANONYMOUS (xvth century)

Over one hundred carols with music are preserved in English fifteenth-century manuscripts. These exciting pieces were written for every occasion, not only Christmas. Their dancelike rhythms, repetitive form, catchy tunes (which usually lie in the lowest part), and mixed Latin and English texts indicate they were designed for popular use rather than for the court. The "Verse" portions sound best when sung by solo voices. The refrain sections, marked "Chorus" in the original, precede and follow each verse, distinguishing the carol from other English forms.

VERSE

1.Owre kynge went forth to Nor- man- dy With
1. Owre kynge went forth to Nor- man- dy With

grace and myght of chy- val- ry; Ther
grace and myght of chy- val- ry; Ther

God for hym wrought merve-lus- - ly; Wher-
God for hym wrought merve-lus- ly; Wher-

fore Eng- londe may calle and
fore Eng- londe may calle and

cry, 'De- o gra- ci - as.
attacca
cry, 'De- o gra- ci - as.'

CHORUS B

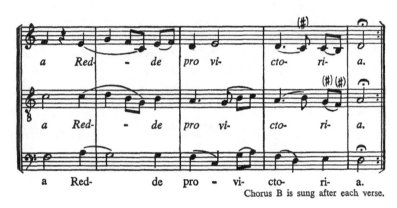

Chorus B is sung after each verse.

2.

He sette a sege, the sothe for
 to say,
To Harflu toune with ryal aray;
That toune he wan and made a
 fray
That Fraunce shal rywe tyl
 domesday;
 Deo gracias.

3.

Than went oure kynge with alle his
 oste
Throwe Fraunce, for alle the Freshe
 boste;
He spared no drede of lest ne
 moste
Tyl he come to Agincourt coste;
 Deo gracias.

4.

Than, forsoth, that knyght comely,
In Agincourt feld he faught manly;
Thorw grace of God most myghty
He had bothe the felde and the
    victory;
    Deo gracias.

5.

There dukys and erlys, lorde and
    barone
Were take and slayne, and that wel
    sone,
And summe were ladde into
    Lundone
With joye and merthe and grete
    renone;
    Deo gracias.

6.

Now gracious God he save oure
    kynge,
His peple, and alle his wel-wyllynge;
Yef hym gode lyfe and gode
    endynge,
That we with merth mowe savely
    synge;
    Deo gracias.

DEO GRACIAS ANGLIA
The Agincourt Carol

Deo gracias Anglia/Redde pro victoria—Render thanks to God, England,
for victory; *Yef*—grant.

NOVA, NOVA

ANONYMOUS (xvth century)

Briskly

T&B (S&A)
f No- va, no- va

'A- ve' fitt ex 'E- va.'

VERSE
T (Bar)
mf 1. Ga- bri- ell of hygh de- gre,

He cam down from the Try- ny-

te, From Na- za- reth to

Ga- la- lye, No- - va,

no- - va,

CHORUS
f No- va, no- va

'A- ve' fitt ex 'E- va.'

66

2.

He mete a maydyn in a place;
He kneled down before her face;
He sayd, 'Hayle, Mary, full of
  grace.'
Nova, nova.

3.

When the maydyn sawe all this,
She was sore abashed, ywys,
Lest that she had done amys;
Nova, nova.

4.

Then sayd the angell, 'Dred not
  you:
Ye shall conceyve in all vertu
A chyld whose name shall be
  Jhesu.'
Nova, nova.

5.

Then sayd the mayd, 'How may
  this be,
Godes son to be born of me?
I know not of manys carnalite.'
Nova, nova.

6.

Then said the angell anon ryght,
'The Holy Gost ys on the plyght;
Ther ys nothyng unpossible to God
  Almyght.'
Nova, nova.

7.

Then sayd the angell anon,
'Ytt ys not fully vi moneth agon
Syth Seynt Elizabeth conceyved
  Seynt Johan.'
Nova, nova.

8.

Then sayd the mayd anon a-hye,
'I am Godes own truly;
Ecce ancilla Domini.'
Nova, nova.

Chorus is sung after each verse.

NOVA, NOVA

Nova, nova 'Ave' fitt ex 'Eva'—News, news, "Hail" is made from "Eve"
(Eve's original sin is transformed into Gabriel's salutation). *Ecce ancilla Domini*—Behold the Lord's handmaiden.

67

NOWEL SYNG WE BOTHE
AL AND SOM

ANONYMOUS (XVth century)

Boisterously and fast

No- wel syng we ___ bothe al ___ and

No- wel syng we bothe al and

som, Now Rex Pa- ci- fi- cus ys ___ y- come.

som, Now Rex Pa- ci- fi- cus ys y- come.

VERSE

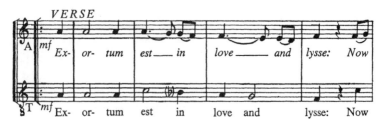

Ex- or- tum est ___ in love ___ and lysse: Now

Ex- or- tum est in love and lysse: Now

68

69

2.

De fructu ventris of Mary bryght:
Bothe God and man in here alyght;
Owte of dysese he dyde us dyght,
 Bothe alle and summe.

3.

Puer natus to us was sent,
To blysse us bought, fro bale us
 blent,
And ellys to wo we hadde ywent,
 Bothe alle and summe.

4.

Lux fulgebit with love and lyght,
In Mary mylde his pynon pyght,
In here toke kynde with manly
 myght,
 Bothe alle and summe.

5.

Gloria tibi ay and blysse:
God unto his grace he us wysse,
The rent of heven that we not
 mysse,
 Bothe alle and summe.

Chorus is sung after each verse.

NOWEL SYNG WE BOTHE AL AND SOM
Rex Pacificus—King of Peace. *Exortum est*—He is born. *De fructu ventris*
—of the fruit of thy womb. *Puer natus*—A Son is born. *Lux fulgebit*—a
light will shine. *Gloria tibi*—Glory to Thee.

lysse—joy; *gysse*—prepare; *dyght*—put; *blent*—took; *his pennon pyght*—set
up his pennant; *wysse*—guide; *rent*—reward.

QUID PETIS O FILI

RICHARD PYGOTT (*c.* 1485-*c.* 1552)

Pygott was master of the choir in Cardinal Wolsey's private chapel and, later, a member of Henry VIIIth's Royal Household Chapel. His lovely carol *Quid petis o fili* appears in a manuscript collection dating from the early 1500's (British Museum Additional Manuscript 31922), which contains vocal and instrumental music written for the court of Henry VIII. Although this piece still uses the verse-refrain form and the macaronic English and Latin text of the medieval carol, its continuous imitative technique marks it as a work of the Renaissance.

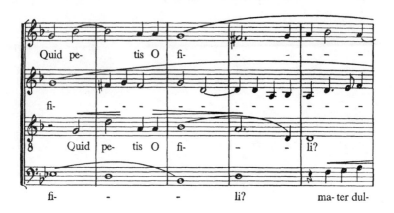

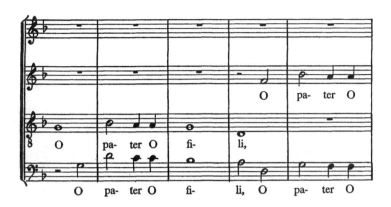

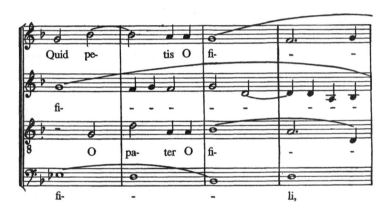

mi- hi plau-sus os- cu- la ____ da ____ da.

os- cu- la ____ da ____ da.

da ____ da.

da da.

VERSE I*
somewhat marked

T *mf* The mo- der full man- er- ly and mek-

B *mf* The mo- der full man- er- ly and mek-

*the verses are best sung by solo voices.

mf lok-yng on her lyt- till son, so laugh-yng in

ly as a mayd lok- yng on her lyt- till son, so laugh-

ly as a mayd

74

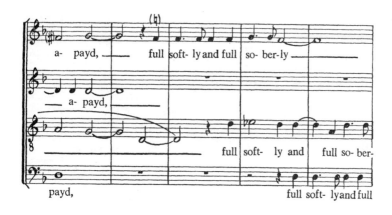

a- payd, ___ full soft- ly and full so- ber- ly ___

_ a- payd, ___

full soft- ly and full so- ber-

payd,   full soft- ly and full

un- to her swete son she said,   un-

un- to her swete ___ son she ___ said,

ly un- - to her son __ she ___ said, __

so- ber-ly   un- to her

REPEAT REFRAIN FROM SIGN

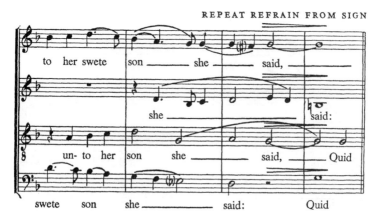

to her swete son ___ she ___ said, ___

she ___ said:

un- to her son she ___ said, ___ Quid

swete son she _____ said: Quid

VERSE II
a bit slower

A — mp I mene this by Ma-ry, oure mak-er's

BAR — mp I mene this by Ma-ry, oure mak-er's

mo-der of myght,

mo-der of myght,

full love-ly look-yng on our Lord, the

full love-ly look-yng on our Lord,

lan-terne of lyght, thus

the lan-terne of lyght, thus sa-yng

sa-yng to our sa-vi-our, this saw I in my syght,

to our sa-vi-our, this saw I in my syght, this

this re-son that I rede you now, I rede

re-son that I rede you now, I rede it

it full ryght.

REFRAIN

full ryght. Quid

77

VERSE III
with motion

S

T

B

mf Mus- yng on her

mf Mus- yng on her man- ers so

mf Mus-yng on her man- ers so my mard

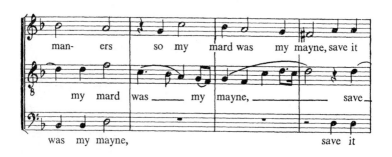

man- ers so my mard was my mayne, save it

my mard was my mayne, save

was my mayne, save it

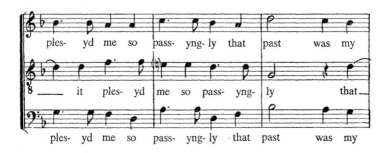

ples- yd me so pass- yng- ly that past was my

it ples- yd me so pass- yng- ly that

ples- yd me so pass- yng- ly that past was my

payn, (-ayn)

pass- yd was my payn, p yet

payn, p yet soft- ly

78

QUID PETIS O FILI

What do you wish, O sweetest
Mother of the Son, ba, ba, ba, ba?
O Father, O Son,
Give me fond kisses, da, da, da, da.

WITH OWT DYSCORDE

KING HENRY VIII (1491-1547)

"For the Kynge hime self beinge miche delited to synge, and Sir Peter Carewe havinge a pleasaunte voyce, the Kynge woulde very often use hyme to synge with hime certeyne songes they called *fremen* songs, as namely, 'By the banke as I lay,' and 'As I walked the wode so wylde,' &c." So writes a chronicler of Henry's music-making which, from all the evidence, was extensive. His instrumental collection was very large, the finest European and English musicians were in his employ, and he composed some rather good *chansons* and instrumental pieces. The two pieces printed here, are in French style and appear in British Museum Add. Ms. 31922.

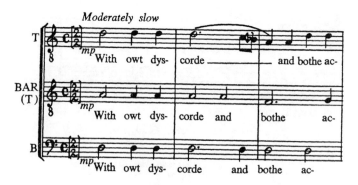

81

WITH OWT DYSCORDE

Wher for now we
that lovers be

       let us now pray.

Onys love sure
ffor to procure

       with owt denay.

Wher love so sewith
ther no hart rewith

       but condyscend.

Yf contrarye
What remedy

       god yt amend.

O MY HART

KING HENRY VIII

A ROBYN, GENTIL ROBYN

WILLIAM CORNYSH (*died c. 1523*)

William Cornysh was composer and poet at the court of Henry VIII. From 1509 to 1523 he held the post of Master of the Children at the Chapel Royal which entailed conducting the choir, composing music for the services, preparing musical activities, and. staging entertainments for the court. *A Robyn* is the setting of a poem by Sir Thomas Wyatt, referred to almost a century later in Shakespeare's *Twelfth Night* (Act IV, sc. 2). Both Cornysh pieces are from the British Museum Ms. already cited.

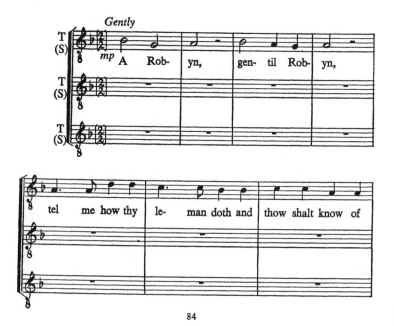

85

myne. *p* A Rob- yn, gen- til Rob-

myne. *mf* My la- dy is un- kynde I wis, a- lac why is she

yn, tel me how thy le- man doth and thow shalt know of

so, she lov'th an-oth- er bet- ter than me and yet she will say

myne. *mf* A Rob- yn, gen- til Rob- yn,

no. *mf* A Rob- yn, gen- til Rob- yn,

tel me how thy le- man doth and thow shalt know of myne.

tel me how thy le- man doth and thow shalt know of myne. *mf* I

A Rob- yn, gen- til Rob- yn,

can not thynk such doub- yl- nes, for I fynd wo- men trew, in

tel me how thy le- man doth and thow shalt know of

faith my la- dy lov'th me well she will change for no

myne. A Rob- yn, gen- til Rob- yn,

new. A Rob- yn, gen- til Rob- yn,

tel me how thy le- man doth and thow shalt know of myne.

tel me how thy le- man doth and thow shalt know of myne.

BLOW THY HORNE HUNTER

WILLIAM CORNYSH

BLOW THY HORNE, HUNTER

Sore thus dere strykyn ys and yet she bled no whytt,
she lay so fayre, I cowde nott mys, lord I was glad of it.
REFRAIN *Now blow thy horne hunter*
and blow thy horne joly hunter.

As I stod under a banke the dere shoffe on the mede,
I stroke her so that downe she sanke, but yet she was not dede.
Now blow thy horne &c.

Ther she gothe, se ye nott, how she gothe over the playne,
And yf ye lust to have a shott, I warrant her barrayne.
Now blow thy horne &c.

He to go and I to go but he ran fast a fore,
I had hym shott and strik the do for I myght shott no more.
Now blow thy horne &c.

To the covert bothe thay went, for I fownd wher she lay,
An arrow in her hanch she hent, for faynte she myght nott bray.
Now blow thy horne &c.

I was wery of the game, I went to tavern to drynk,
now the construcyon on the same, what do yow meane or thynk.
Now blow thy horne &c.

Here I leve and mak an end now of this hunters lore,
I thynk his bow ys well unbent, hys bolt may fle no more.
Now blow thy horne &c.

GLORIA

JOHN TAVERNER (c. 1495-1545)

Taverner's liturgical works are a monumental contribution to early sixteenth-century English music. The *Western Wynde* Mass, from which this *Gloria* is taken, is based on the song of that name. This is a splendid example of Taverner's art: the ornate counterpoint enmeshes the ever-present melody in a polyphonic web without, however, obscuring the song-like quality of the composition. The words *Gloria in excelsis Deo* are not set, since it was Renaissance practice to have the priest intone them.

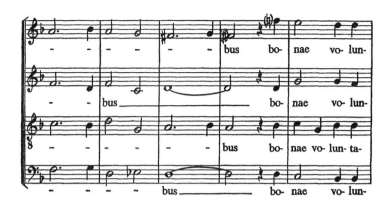

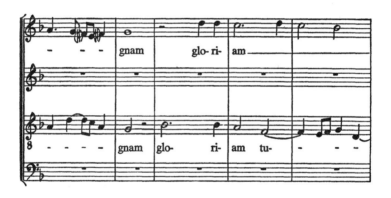

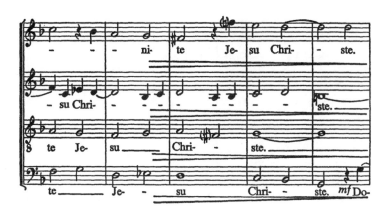

GLORIA

(Glory to God in the highest) And on earth peace to men of good will. We praise Thee. We bless Thee. We adore Thee. We glorify Thee. We give thanks to Thee for Thy great glory. O Lord God, heavenly king, God the Father almighty. O Lord, the only-begotten son, Jesus Christ. Lord God, Lamb of God, Son of the Father.

EDITOR'S NOTE: The following verse is the secular text to the melody as it appears in Brit. Mus. Ms. App. 58:

> Westron wynde when wyll thow blow
> the small rayne down can rayne
> Cryst yf my love wer in my armys
> And I yn my bed Agayne.

AGNUS DEI

THOMAS TALLIS (c. 1505-1585)

"He serv'd long Tyme in Chappell with grete prayse,
Fower Sovereygnes Reygnes (a thing not often seen)
I mean Kyng Henry and Prince Edward's Dayes,
Quene Mary and Elizabeth our Quene."

from Tallis' epitaph

Tallis' works represent the full flowering of Renaissance music in England. His greatest compositions were those written for the Latin Service —works charged with deep emotion and executed with the greatest craftsmanship. This music, while influenced by the continental masters, is unmistakably in the English tradition. The *Agnus Dei* is from his Mass for four voices, probably an early work; the *Salvator mundi* is from *Cantiones sacrae,* a collection of motets by Tallis and Byrd, printed in 1575.

98

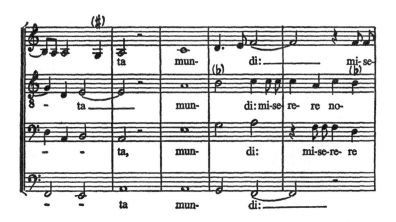

AGNUS DEI

Lamb of God, who takest away the sins of the world, have mercy on us.
Lamb of God, who takest away the sins of the world, have mercy on us.
Lamb of God, who takest away the sins of the world, grant us peace.

SALVATOR MUNDI

THOMAS TALLIS

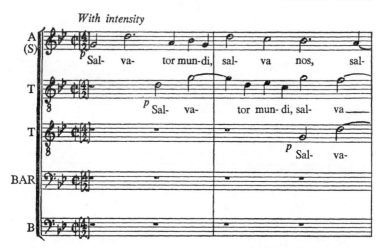

107

SALVATOR MUNDI

Saviour of the world, save us. Thou who hast redeemed us by the Cross
and thy blood, help us, we pray thee, our God.

J.N.

SUSANNA FAYRE
SOMETIME ASSAULTED WAS

WILLIAM BYRD (1543-1623)

The most esteemed and prolific English composer of his time, William Byrd represents the late Renaissance style at its very best. He wrote in all the forms and for all the media known to the sixteenth century: madrigals; solo songs; music for viol ensemble; solo instrumental pieces for organ, lute, and harpsichord; anthems and Services for the English Church; Latin masses and motets. The great variety of his output is equaled by few musicians of any period. The Penitential motet, *Emendemus in melius*, is from *Cantiones sacrae* (1575). The settings of the "Susanna and the Elders" story and the description of Dido's death are from *Songs of Sundrie Natures* (1589).

110

not by tend-er love, if not by tend-er love, by force and

love, if not by tend-er love, by force and

might, by force and might, by force and

f might, *p* to whom shee saide, to whom shee saide, If I

f might, *p* to whom shee saide, if I your sute

f might, *p* to whom shee saide, to whom shee saide, If

your sute de- nie, you will mee false- lie ac-

de- nie, your sute de- nie, you will mee false-

I your sute de- nie, de- nie, you will mee

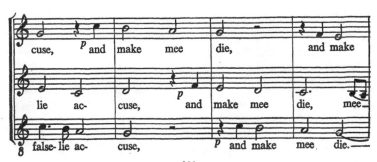

cuse, *p* and make mee die, and make

lie ac- cuse, *p* and make mee die, mee

false-lie ac- cuse, *p* and make mee die.

111

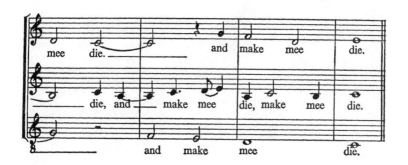

mee die. _____ and make mee die.

_____ die, and _____ make mee die, make mee die.

_____ and make mee die.

mf And if I graunt to that which you re- quest, my

mf And if I graunt to that which you re-

mf And if I graunt

chas- ti- tie shall then de- flour- ed bee,

quest, my chas- ti- tie shall

to that which you ___ re- quest, my

shall then de- flour- ed bee, my chas-

then de- flour- ed bee, my chas- ti- tie shall

chas- ti- tie shall then de- flour- ed bee,

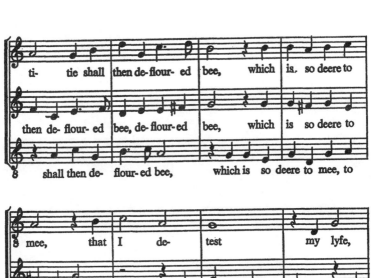

113

114

EMENDEMUS IN MELIUS

WILLIAM BYRD

pec- ca- vi- mus ti- - - bi. ᵖAd- iu-

pec- ca- vi- mus ti- bi. ᵖAd- iu-

pec- ca- vi- mus ti- - - bi. ᵖAd- iu-

pec- ca- vi- mus ti- bi, ᵖAd- iu-

.pec- ca- vi- mus ti- bi. ᵖAd- iu-

va nos, De- - us sa- lu-

va nos, De- - us sa- lu- ta- ris no-

va nos, De- us sa- lu- ta- ris

va nos, De- us sa- lu- ta- ris no- ster,

va nos, De- us sa- lu-

ta- ris no- - - - ster, ᶠet pro-

ster, sa- lu- ta- ris no- ster, ᶠet pro-

no- ster, no- - ster, ᶠet pro-

sa- lu- ta- ris no- ster, ᶠet pro-

ta- ris no- ster, ᶠet pro-

118

EMENDEMUS IN MELIUS

Let us make amends for sinning in ignorance; lest suddenly overtaken by the day of death, we seek space for penance, and are not able to find it. Attend, O Lord, and have mercy, for we have sinned against Thee. Help us, O God, our Saviour: and for the honor of Thy name, O Lord, deliver us.

J.N.

WHEN FIRST BY FORCE
OF FATALL DESTENIE

WILLIAM BYRD

125

ABOUT THE MAY POLE

THOMAS MORLEY (1557-1603?)
The Italian vogue that overtook England during Elizabeth's rule brought
with it the musical fashions current in Venice and Rome. As editor,
Morley popularized the madrigal, publishing collections of music by Italy's
leading composers. His own madrigals, ballets, and canzonets are pat-
terned after Italian forms, but have a distinctly Elizabethan flavor that
distinguishes them from their models. The pieces here are from Morley's
First Booke of Balletts (1595), *Canzonets...to three voyces* (1593), and
Canzonets to two voyces (1595).

128

129

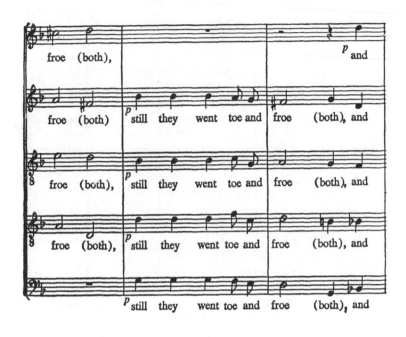

froe (both), *p* and

froe (both) *p* still they went toe and froe (both), and

froe (both), *p* still they went toe and froe (both), and

froe (both), *p* still they went toe and froe (both), and

p still they went toe and froe (both), and

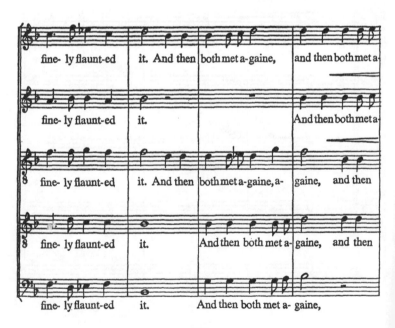

fine- ly flaunt-ed it. And then both met a-gaine, and then both met a-

fine- ly flaunt-ed it. And then both met a-

fine- ly flaunt-ed it. And then both met a-gaine, a- gaine, and then

fine- ly flaunt-ed it. And then both met a- gaine, and then

fine- ly flaunt-ed it. And then both met a- gaine,

ABOUT THE MAY POLE

VERSE II

The Sheperds and the Nimphes them round enclosed had,
Wondring with what facilitie,
About they turnd them in such strange agilitie. Fa la la.
And still when they unlosed had,
With words full of delight they gently kissed them,
And thus sweetly to sing they never missed them.

LEAVE ALAS THIS TORMENTING

THOMAS MORLEY

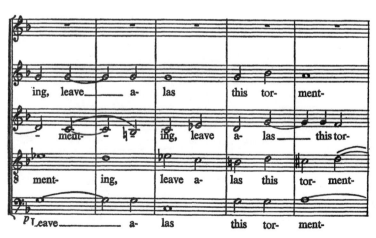

134

135

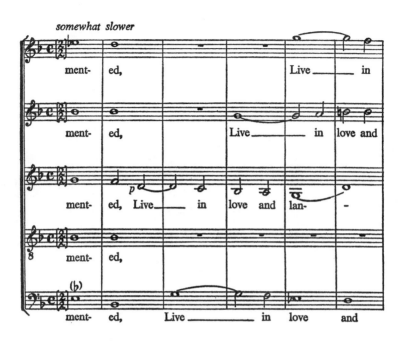

137

guish, ᵖlive _____ in love and lan-

_____ in love and lan- guish, live _____ in

guish, live_____ in love and lan- -

ᵖlive_____ in love and lan- - guish, live in

_____ ᵖlive_____ in love and

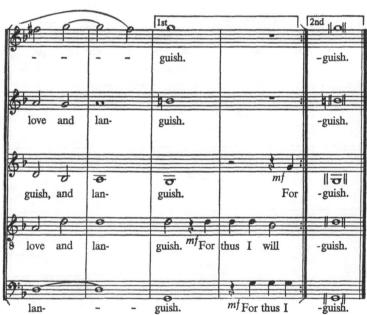

1st ── guish. 2nd -guish.

love and lan- guish. -guish.

guish, and lan- guish. *mf* For -guish.

love and lan- guish. *mf*For thus I will -guish.

lan- - - guish. *mf* For thus I -guish.

CEASE MINE EYES

THOMAS MORLEY

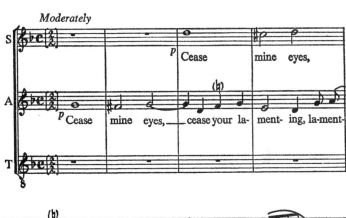

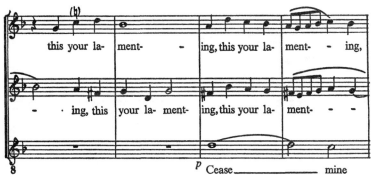

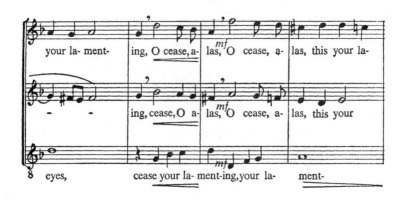

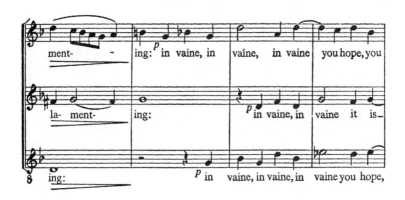

140

141

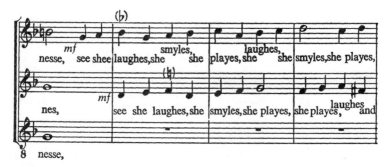

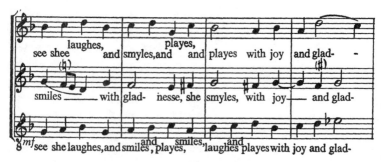

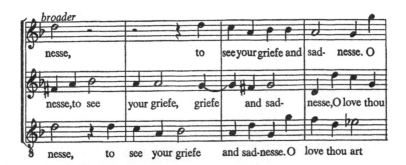

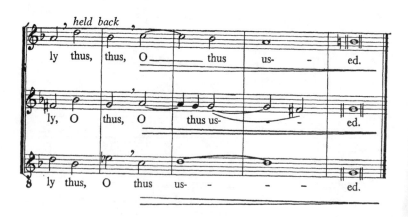

I GOE BEFORE MY DARLING

THOMAS MORLEY

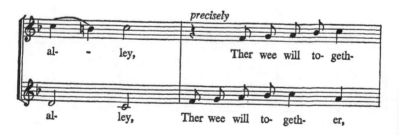

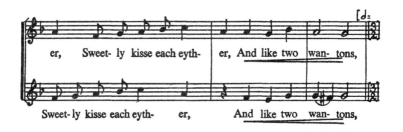

er, Sweet- ly kisse each eyth-   er, And like two wan- tons,

Sweet-ly kisse each eyth-   er,   And like two wan- tons,

ƒ Dal- ly dal- ly dal-   ly dal- ly   dal- ly dal- ly dal-

ƒ Dal-   ly dal- ly   dal- ly dal- ly dal-

ly   dal- ly dal- ly dal- ly   dal-   ly dal- ly

ly   dal- ly dal- ly dal- ly dal-   ly   dal-   ly

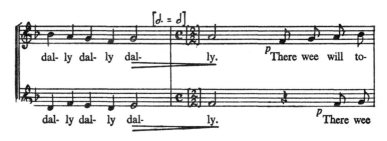

dal- ly dal- ly   dal-   ly.   ᵖThere wee will to-

dal- ly dal- ly   dal-   ly.   ᵖThere wee

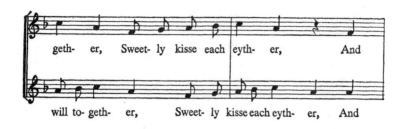

geth- er, Sweet- ly kisse each eyth- er, And

will to- geth- er, Sweet- ly kisse each eyth- er, And

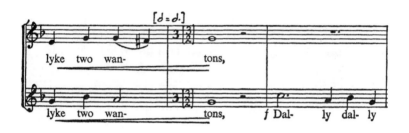

lyke two wan- tons,

lyke two wan- tons, *f* Dal- ly dal- ly

f Dal- ly dal- ly dal- ly dal- ly dal- ly dal- ly

dal- ly dal- ly dal- ly dal- ly dal- ly

dal- ly dal- ly dal- ly dal- ly dal- ly dal- ly dal- ly.

dal- ly dal- ly dal- ly dal- ly dal- ly dal- ly dal- ly dal- ly.

TOSSE NOT MY SOULE

JOHN DOWLAND (1563-1626)

Dowland was the most famous lutenist-composer of his time. His instrumental music and airs were known in England and on the continent, since he traveled widely and performed in Italy, Germany, France, Denmark, and the Low Countries. Dowland's magnificent songs, his virtuoso fantasies for lute, and superb dances for instrumental ensemble have no peers in late sixteenth and early seventeenth-century music. Included here are two songs from his second (1600) and third (1603) song books, in Dowland's own setting for vocal quartet. The lute part, which appears under the solo line in the original publication, is not reprinted here.

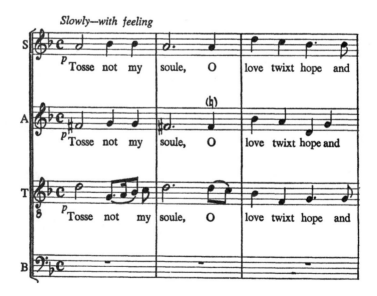

149

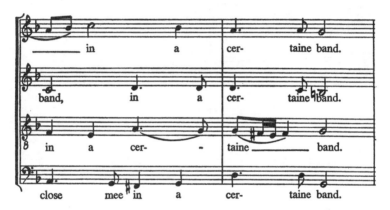

L'envoy

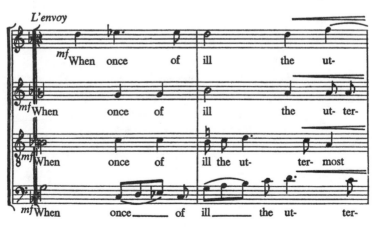

151

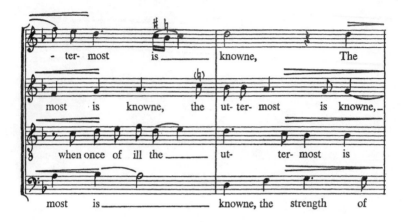

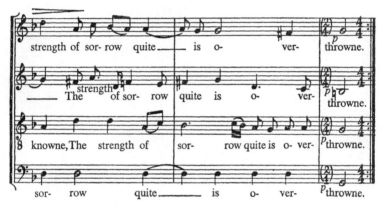

TOSSE NOT MY SOULE

VERSE II

Take mee *Assurance* to thy blissfull holde,
Or thou *Despaire* unto thy darkest Cell,
Each hath full rest, the one in joyes enrolde,
Th'other, in that hee feares no more, is well:
When once of ill the uttermost is knowne,
The strength of sorrow quite is overthrowne.

WHAT IF I NEVER SPEEDE

JOHN DOWLAND

feede that ___ can no losse re- paire.
prove I ___ can com- mand my hart.

But if she will pit- tie my de- sire, and ___

But if she will pit- tie, pit- tie, pit- tie my de- sire,

But if she will pit- tie my de- sire, and my

But if she will pit- tie my de- sire, and my

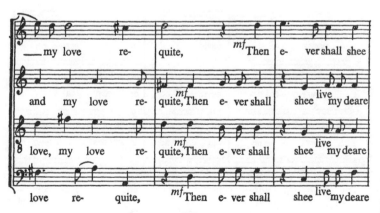

___ my love re- quite, *mf* Then e- ver shall shee

and my love re- quite, *mf* Then e- ver shall shee live my deare

love, my love re- quite, *mf* Then e- ver shall shee live my deare

love re- quite, *mf* Then e- ver shall shee live my deare

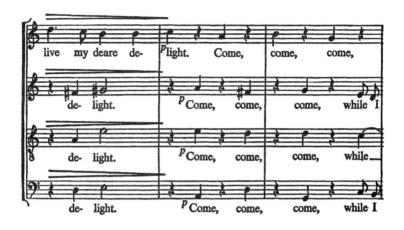

VERSE II

Oft have I dream'd of joy
   yet I never felt the sweete,
But tired with annoy,
   my griefs each other greete.
Oft have I left my hope,
   as a wretch by fate forlorne,
But Love aims at one scope,
   and lost will stil returne:
He that once loves with a true desire
   never can depart,
  For *Cupid* is the king of every hart.
   Come, come &c.

THUS SAITH MY CLORIS BRIGHT

JOHN WILBYE (1574-1638)

It is a pity that so little of Wilbye's music survives, because his two books of madrigals and a handful of sacred pieces reveal him as a most sensitive musician. While he was completely caught up in the current Italian vogue, his use of that style rises above mere imitation: such devices as word-painting and sequence are never employed for their own sake. The two pieces included here are from his first set of madrigals (1598), published while Wilbye was employed as household musician to the family of Sir Thomas Kytson.

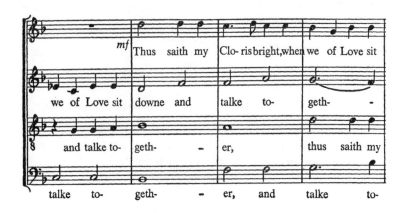

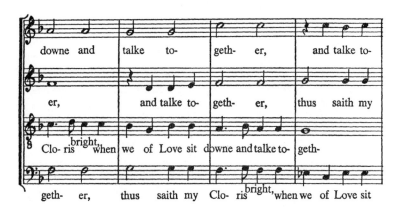

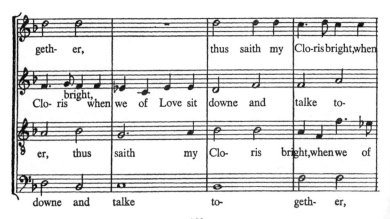

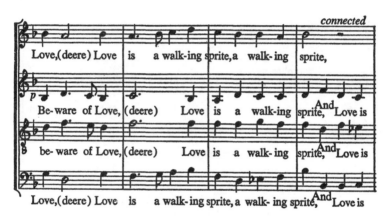

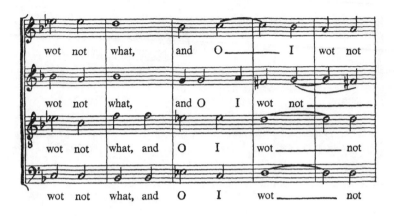

wot not what, and O   I wot not

wot not what, and O I wot not

wot not what, and O I wot not

wot not what, and O I wot not

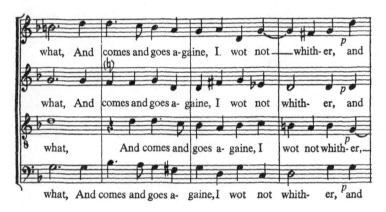

what, And comes and goes a-gaine, I. wot not whith-er, *p* and

what, And comes and goes a- gaine, I wot not whith- er, *p* and

what, And comes and goes a- gaine, I wot not whith-er, *p*

what, And comes and goes a- gaine, I wot not whith- er, *P* and

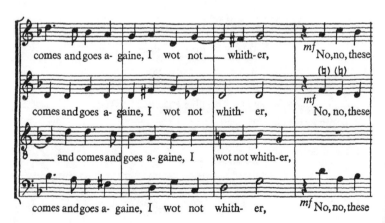

comes and goes a- gaine, I wot not whith-er, *mf* No, no, these

comes and goes a- gaine, I wot not whith- er, *mf* No, no, these

and comes and goes a- gaine, I wot not whith-er,

comes and goes a- gaine, I wot not whith- er, *mf* No, no, these

are but bugs to | breed a- maz- | ing, No, no, these | are but bugs· to

are but bugs to | breed a- maz- | ing,

No, no, these

mf No, no, these | are but bugs to | breed a- maz-

are but bugs to breed a- maz- ing, to breed a-

breed a- maz- ing, *f* For

are but bugs to breed a- maz- ing,

ing, to breed a- maz- ing, *f* For in her

maz- ing, *f* For in her

in her eies I saw his torch light blaz- ing.

f For in her eies I saw his torch light blaz- ing.

eies I saw his torch light blaz- ing.

eies I saw his torch light blaz- ing.

ALAS, WHAT HOPE OF SPEEDING

JOHN WILBYE

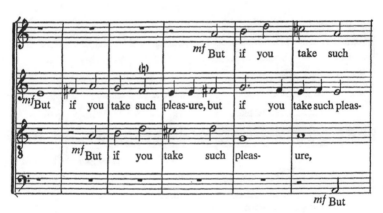

joy hope and joy my treas- ure, Of hope and joy, of
hope and joy, _____ my treas- - - ure, of hope and
joy my treas- ure, my treas- - ure, of hope and joy my
hope and joy my treas- ure, of hope and

hope and joy_____ my treas- ure, By de-ceipt to be-reave me,
joy my treas- ure, By de-ceipt, to be-reave me,
treas- ure, my treas- ure, By de-ceipt, to be-
joy my treas- ure, By de- ceipt, to be-

to be- reave me, by de-ceipt to be-reave me, to be- reave
by de- ceipt, to be- reave me, by de- ceipt to be-
reave _____ me, by de-ceipt _____ to be-reave
reave me, by de- ceipt to be- reave

me, *f* by de- ceipt to be- reave me, *p* by de- ceipt, by de- ceipt—

reave me, by de- ceipt to be- reave me, *p* by de- ceipt to be-

me, *f* by de- ceipt to be- reave me, *p* by de- ceipt to be-

me, *f* by de- ceipt to be- reave me, *p* by de- ceipt to be-

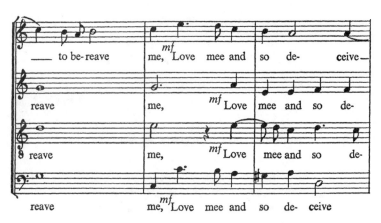

— to be- reave me, *mf* Love mee and so de- ceive—

reave me, *mf* Love mee and so de-

reave me, *mf* Love mee and so de-

reave me, *mf* Love mee and so de- ceive

— mee, *f* Love—mee and so de- ceive ——— mee.

ceive mee, ——— *f* Love mee and so de- ceive mee.

ceive mee, *f* Love mee and so de- ceive mee.

mee, *f* Love—mee and so de- ceive mee.

TAN TA RA RAN TAN TANT

THOMAS WEELKES (*c.* 1575-1623)

Tan ta ra and the lament on the death of Morley are from Weelkes'
Ayeres or Phantasticke Spirites (1608). This was the last of four volumes
of secular music published during the lifetime of this excellent composer.
He held the position of organist-composer at Chichester Cathedral and
wrote extensively for the Service, though very little of this music has
survived in complete form. Weelkes was strongly influenced by the Italians
and he often used chromatic devices and harmonies that were quite ex-
treme by English standards. The two pieces which follow show him in
both his lightest and most serious moods,

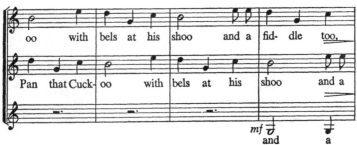

DEATH HATH DEPRIVED MEE

A remembrance of my friend M. Thomas Morley

THOMAS WEELKES

171

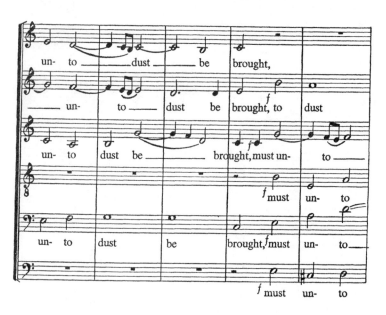

WHAT SHALL I PART THUS

GEORGE KIRBYE (*c.* 1570-1634)

Kirbye, one of the lesser-known Madrigalists, wrote almost entirely in the Italian manner. The present piece appears in his only publication, *The First Set of English Madrigalls* (1597). The generally high *tessitura* makes for a very intense vocal sound which is most effective and moving.

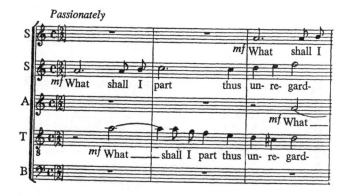

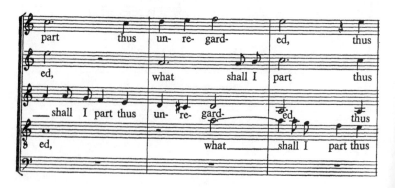

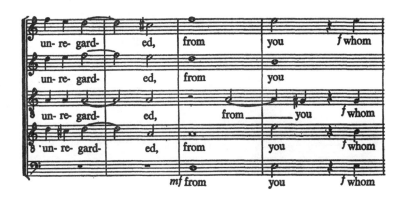

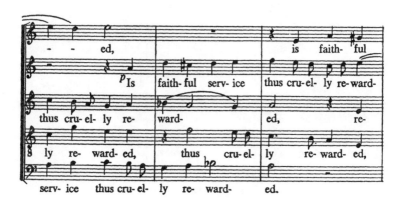

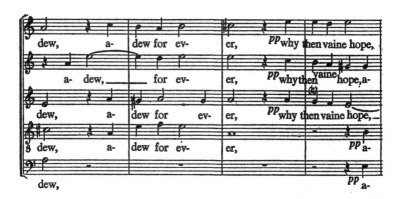

*Soprano parts interchange on repeat.

179

WEEPE FORTH YOUR TEARES,
AND DOE LAMENT

A Mourning Song in memory of Prince Henry

JOHN WARD (*flourished* 1613)

John Ward's *Mourning Song* was one of a number of laments composed for the funeral, in 1612, of the young Prince of Wales, son of King James I. From a contemporary description we learn that the music for the funeral procession was sung by the men and children of the king's chapel accompanied by various instruments. *Weepe forth your teares* appears as the final piece in Ward's only set of madrigals published in 1613. The title page of this collection suggests the use of instruments with the phrase "... Apt both for Viols and Voyces ..."

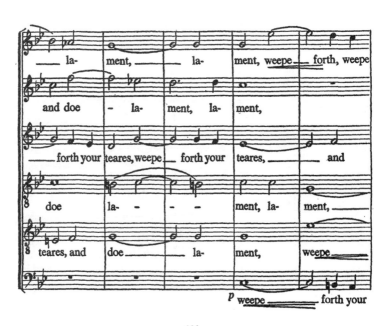

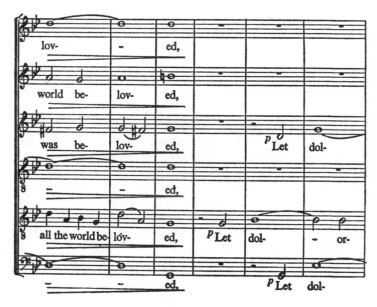

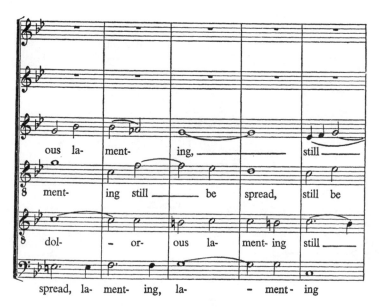

184

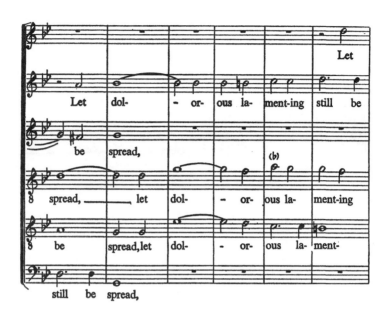

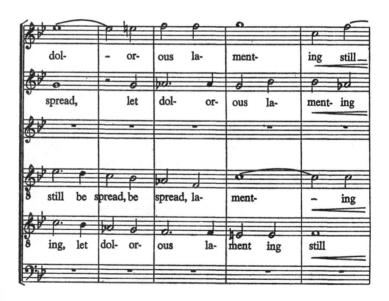

185

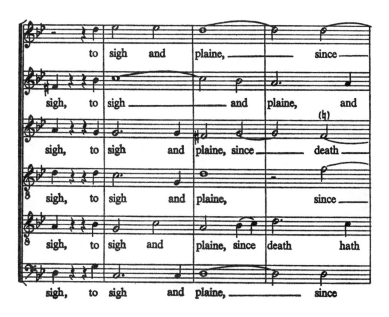

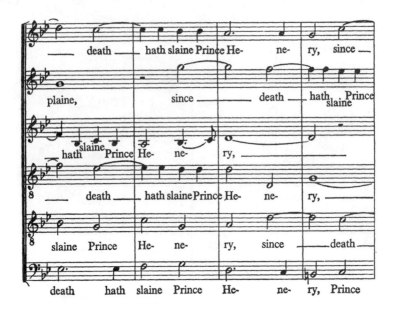

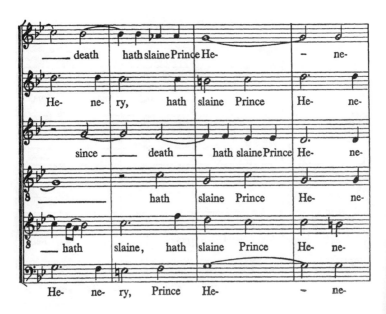

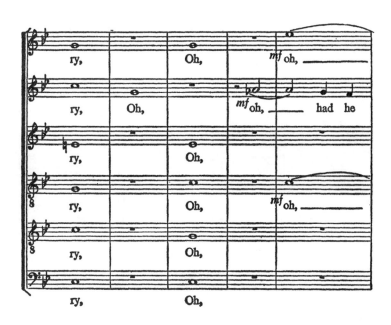

189

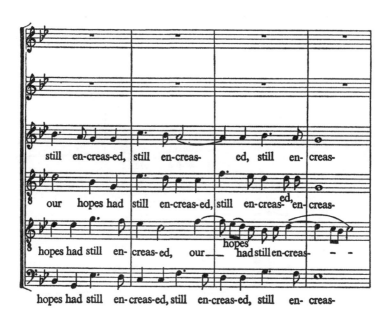

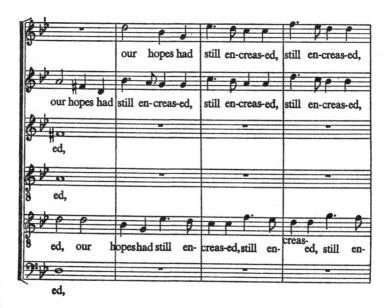

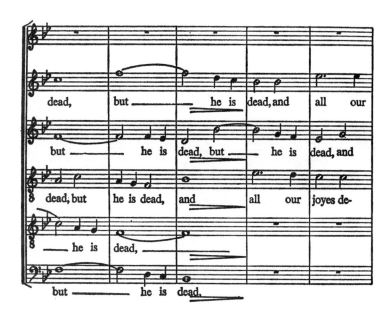

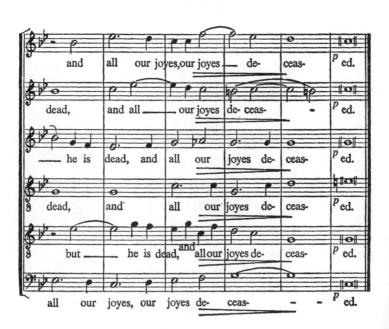

O LORD, INCREASE MY FAITH

ORLANDO GIBBONS (1583-1625)

Gibbons, less influenced by the Italians than his contemporaries, is the continuer of the insular tradition represented by Tallis and Byrd in Tudor times. His writings include a set of five-part madrigals, keyboard pieces, music for viols, and sacred works for the English Service. He became a member of the Chapel Royal in 1605 and was the organist of Westminster Abbey during the last two years of his life. Gibbons' works have great depth and grandeur and are marked with an individuality that sets him apart from the other composers of Jacobean England.

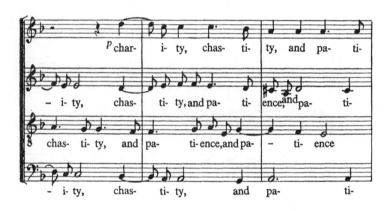

held back

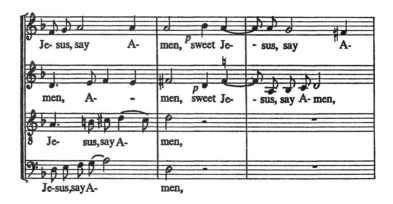

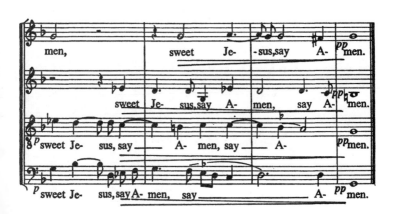

OKEN LEAVES

A round for three voices

THOMAS RAVENSCROFT (1592?-1635?)

Ravenscroft's *Pammelia* (1609), *Deuteromelia* (1609), and *Mellismata* (1611) exemplify the rarely notated popular music of the sixteenth century. This music gives a picture of Elizabethan life quite different from the elegant one reflected by sophisticated composers of Tudor court and chapel. For these collections Ravenscroft arranged rounds and part-songs with a great variety of texts: sacred, ribald, and nonsense songs, ballads, and street cries. Many of the tunes and texts originate before Elizabeth's reign but remain current, in corrupted form, into the seventeenth century.

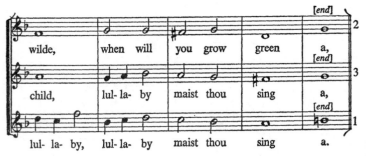

*originally a fifth lower

NEW OYSTERS

A round for three voices

THOMAS RAVENSCROFT

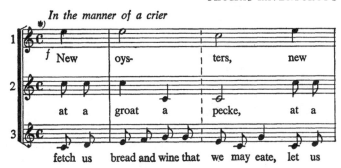

In the manner of a crier

1 — *f* New oys- ters, new

2 — at a groat a pecke, at a

3 — fetch us bread and wine that we may eate, let us

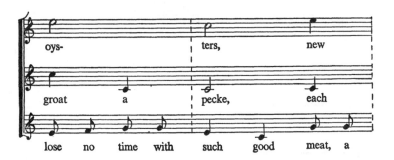

oys- ters, new

groat a pecke, each

lose no time with such good meat, a

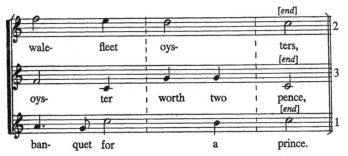

wale- fleet oys- ters, [end]

oys- ter worth two pence, [end]

ban- quet for a prince. [end]

*This round is in a mixed meter, alternating between two-quarter and three-quarter time.

199

O LORD TURNE NOT AWAY THY FACE

A round for four voices

THOMAS RAVENSCROFT

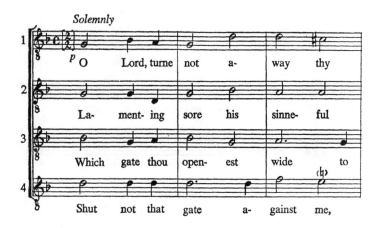

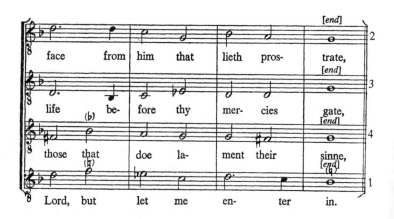

BLOW THY HORNE THOU JOLLY HUNTER

A round for four voices

THOMAS RAVENSCROFT

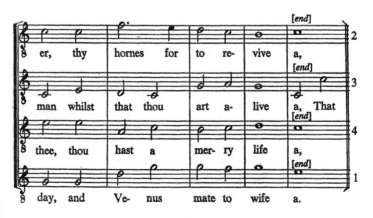

WEE BE THREE POORE MARINERS

THOMAS RAVENSCROFT

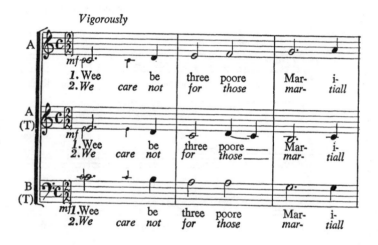

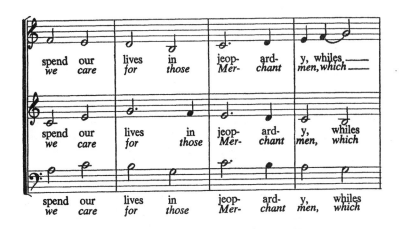

spend our lives in jeop- ard- y, whiles, men, which

we care for those Mer- chant

spend our lives in jeop- ard- y, whiles

we care for those Mer- chant men, which

spend our lives in jeop- ard- y, whiles

we care for those Mer- chant men, which

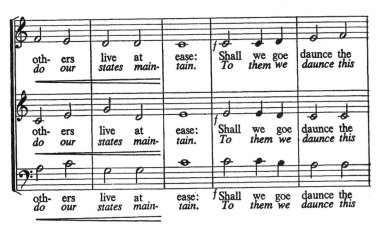

oth- ers live at ease: Shall we goe daunce the

do our states main- tain. To them we daunce this

oth- ers live at ease: Shall we goe daunce the

do our states main- tain. To them we daunce this

oth- ers live at ease: Shall we goe daunce the

do our states main- tain. To them we daunce this

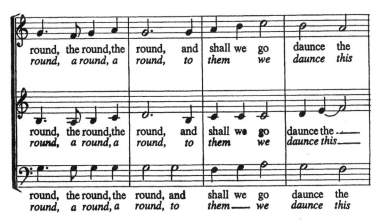

round, the round, the round, and shall we go daunce the

round, a round, a round, to them we daunce this

round, the round, the round, and shall we go daunce the

round, a round, a round, to them we daunce this

round, the round, the round, and shall we go daunce the

round, a round, a round, to them we daunce this

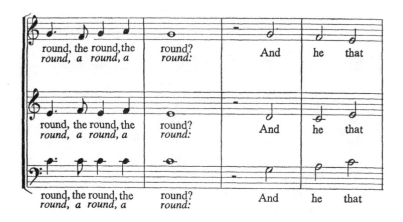

round, the round, the | round? | And | he | that
round, a round, a | *round:*

round, the round, the | round? | And | he | that
round, a round, a | *round:*

round, the round, the | round? | And | he | that
round, a round, a | *round:*

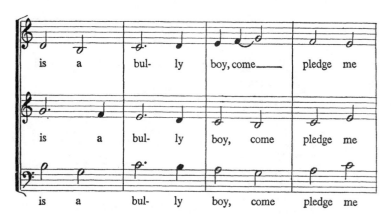

is | a | bul- | ly | boy, come_____ | pledge me

is | a | bul- | ly | boy, | come | pledge me

is | a | bul- | ly | boy, | come | pledge me

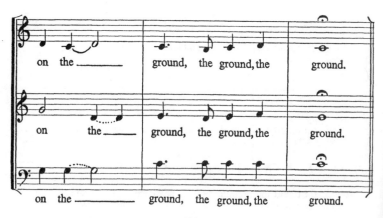

on the_____ | ground, the ground, the | ground.

on the_____ | ground, the ground, the | ground.

on the_____ | ground, the ground, the | ground.

HE THAT WILL AN ALE-HOUSE KEEPE

A round for three voices

THOMAS RAVENSCROFT

He that will an Ale- house keep, must
Cham- ber and a feath- er Bed, a
hay no- ny no- ny, hey no- ny no, hey

have three things in store, a
Chim- ney and a hey no- ny no- ny,
no- ny no, hey no- ny no.

REMEMBER O THOU MAN

A Christmas Carroll

THOMAS RAVENSCROFT

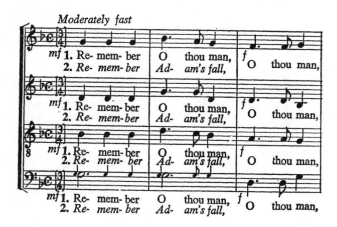

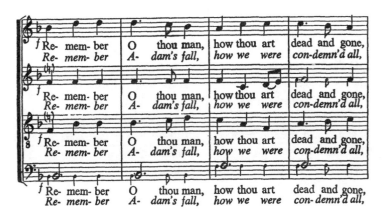

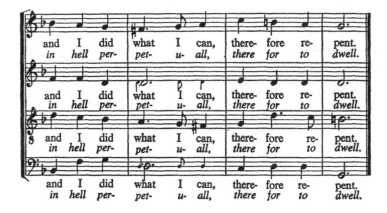

REMEMBER O THOU MAN

3.	4.
Remember God's goodnesse	The Angels all did sing,
O thou man, O thou man	O thou man, O thou man,
Remember God's goodnesse	The Angels all did sing
And his promise made.	Upon Shepheards hill.
Remember God's goodnesse,	The Angels all did sing
How he sent his son doubtlesse	Praises to our heavenly King,
Our sinnes for to redresse,	And peace to man living
be not affraid.	with a good will.

5.

The shepheards amazed was,
 O thou man, O thou man,
The shepheards amazed was
To heare the Angels sing,
The shepheards amazed was
How it should come to passe
That Christ our Messias
 should be our King.

6.

To Bethlem did they goe,
 O thou man, O thou man,
To Bethlem did they go
The shepheards three,
To Bethlem did they goe
To see where it were so or no,
Whether Christ were borne or no
 to set men free.

7.

As the Angels before did say,
 O thou man, O thou man,
As the Angels before did say,
So it came to passe,
As the Angels before did say,
They found a babe where as it lay
In a manger wrapt in hay,
 so poore he was.

8.

In Bethlem he was borne,
 O thou man, O thou man,
In Bethlem he was borne,
For mankind sake,
In Bethlem he was borne
For us that were forlorne,
And therefore tooke no scorne
 our flesh to take.

9.

Give thanks to God alway,
 O thou man, O thou man,
Give thanks to God alway
With heart most joyfully,
Give thanks to God alway,
For this our happy day,
Let all men sing and say
 holy, holy.

NUNC DIMITTIS

THOMAS TOMKINS (1572-1656)

Though he lived past the middle of the seventeenth century, Tomkins' music is very much a part of the late Tudor tradition and shows the influence of his teacher, William Byrd. He has left us a fine book of secular and sacred madrigals (1622), instrumental music—primarily for keyboard—and a large body of liturgical works published posthumously in 1668 as *Musica Deo Sacra*. The *Nunc Dimittis* is from the First Evensong Service in that collection. Our edition does not include the skeletal organ part in the original.

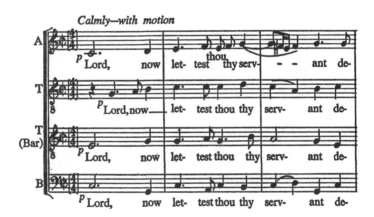

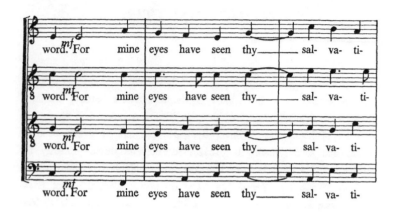

word. *mf* For mine eyes have seen thy_____ sal- va- ti-

word. *mf* For mine eyes have seen thy_____ sal- va- ti-

word. *mf* For mine eyes have seen thy_____ sal- va- ti-

word. *mf* For mine eyes have seen thy_____ sal- va- ti-

on, which thou hast pre- par- ed be- fore the

on, which thou hast pre-par- ed be- fore the

on, which thou hast pre-par- ed be- fore the

on, which thou hast pre- par- ed be- fore the

face of all peo- ple; *p* To be a light to

face of_____all peo- ple; *p* To be a light to

face of all _____ peo- ple; *p* To be a light to

face of all _____ peo- ple; *p* To be a light to

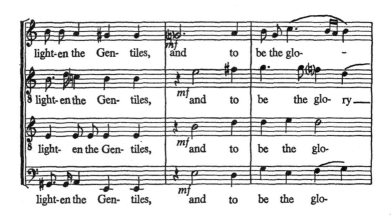

light-en the Gen- tiles, *mf* and to be the glo- -

mf light-en the Gen- tiles, and to be the glo- ry

light- en the Gen- tiles, *mf* and to be the glo-

light-en the Gen- tiles, *mf* and to be the glo-

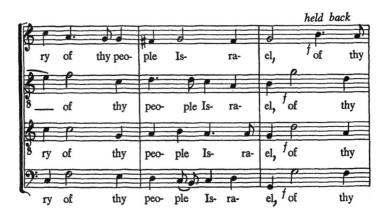

held back

ry of thy peo- ple Is- ra- el, *f* of thy

____ of thy peo- ple Is- ra- el, *f* of thy

ry of thy peo- ple Is- ra- el, *f* of thy

ry of thy peo- ple Is- ra- el, *f* of thy

stronger and broad

peo-ple Is- ra- el. Glo- ry be to ___ the Fa- ther

peo- ple Is- ra- el. Glo- ry be to ___ the Fa- ther

peo- ple Is- ra- el. Glo- ry be to ___ the Fa- ther

peo- ple Is- ra- el. Glo- ry be to ___ the Fa- ther

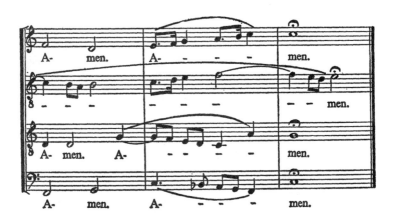

INDEXES

TITLE INDEX

COMPOSER INDEX

216

VOCAL PART INDEX

Music for One Voice

Music for Two Voices

Music for Three Voices

Music for Four Voices

Music for Five Voices

Music for Six Voices

A CATALOG OF SELECTED DOVER
BOOKS IN ALL FIELDS OF INTEREST

CONCERNING THE SPIRITUAL IN ART, Wassily Kandinsky. Pioneering work by father of abstract art. Thoughts on color theory, nature of art. Analysis of earlier masters. 12 illustrations. 80pp. of text. 5⅜ x 8½.   23411-8

ANIMALS: 1,419 Copyright-Free Illustrations of Mammals, Birds, Fish, Insects, etc., Jim Harter (ed.). Clear wood engravings present, in extremely lifelike poses, over 1,000 species of animals. One of the most extensive pictorial sourcebooks of its kind. Captions. Index. 284pp. 9 x 12.   23766-4

CELTIC ART: The Methods of Construction, George Bain. Simple geometric techniques for making Celtic interlacements, spirals, Kells-type initials, animals, humans, etc. Over 500 illustrations. 160pp. 9 x 12. (Available in U.S. only.)   22923-8

AN ATLAS OF ANATOMY FOR ARTISTS, Fritz Schider. Most thorough reference work on art anatomy in the world. Hundreds of illustrations, including selections from works by Vesalius, Leonardo, Goya, Ingres, Michelangelo, others. 593 illustrations. 192pp. 7⅛ x 10¼.   20241-0

CELTIC HAND STROKE-BY-STROKE (Irish Half-Uncial from "The Book of Kells"): An Arthur Baker Calligraphy Manual, Arthur Baker. Complete guide to creating each letter of the alphabet in distinctive Celtic manner. Covers hand position, strokes, pens, inks, paper, more. Illustrated. 48pp. 8¼ x 11.   24336-2

EASY ORIGAMI, John Montroll. Charming collection of 32 projects (hat, cup, pelican, piano, swan, many more) specially designed for the novice origami hobbyist. Clearly illustrated easy-to-follow instructions insure that even beginning papercrafters will achieve successful results. 48pp. 8¼ x 11.   27298-2

THE COMPLETE BOOK OF BIRDHOUSE CONSTRUCTION FOR WOOD-WORKERS, Scott D. Campbell. Detailed instructions, illustrations, tables. Also data on bird habitat and instinct patterns. Bibliography. 3 tables. 63 illustrations in 15 figures. 48pp. 5¼ x 8½.   24407-5

BLOOMINGDALE'S ILLUSTRATED 1886 CATALOG: Fashions, Dry Goods and Housewares, Bloomingdale Brothers. Famed merchants' extremely rare catalog depicting about 1,700 products: clothing, housewares, firearms, dry goods, jewelry, more. Invaluable for dating, identifying vintage items. Also, copyright-free graphics for artists, designers. Co-published with Henry Ford Museum & Greenfield Village. 160pp. 8¼ x 11.   25780-0

HISTORIC COSTUME IN PICTURES, Braun & Schneider. Over 1,450 costumed figures in clearly detailed engravings—from dawn of civilization to end of 19th century. Captions. Many folk costumes. 256pp. 8⅜ x 11¾.   23150-X

THE BEST TALES OF HOFFMANN, E. T. A. Hoffmann. 10 of Hoffmann's most important stories: "Nutcracker and the King of Mice," "The Golden Flowerpot," etc. 458pp. 5⅜ x 8½. 21793-0

FROM FETISH TO GOD IN ANCIENT EGYPT, E. A. Wallis Budge. Rich detailed survey of Egyptian conception of "God" and gods, magic, cult of animals, Osiris, more. Also, superb English translations of hymns and legends. 240 illustrations. 545pp. 5⅜ x 8½. 25803-3

FRENCH STORIES/CONTES FRANÇAIS: A Dual-Language Book, Wallace Fowlie. Ten stories by French masters, Voltaire to Camus: "Micromegas" by Voltaire; "The Atheist's Mass" by Balzac; "Minuet" by de Maupassant; "The Guest" by Camus, six more. Excellent English translations on facing pages. Also French-English vocabulary list, exercises, more. 352pp. 5⅜ x 8½. 26443-2

CHICAGO AT THE TURN OF THE CENTURY IN PHOTOGRAPHS: 122 Historic Views from the Collections of the Chicago Historical Society, Larry A. Viskochil. Rare large-format prints offer detailed views of City Hall, State Street, the Loop, Hull House, Union Station, many other landmarks, circa 1904-1913. Introduction. Captions. Maps. 144pp. 9⅜ x 12¼. 24656-6

OLD BROOKLYN IN EARLY PHOTOGRAPHS, 1865-1929, William Lee Younger. Luna Park, Gravesend race track, construction of Grand Army Plaza, moving of Hotel Brighton, etc. 157 previously unpublished photographs. 165pp. 8⅞ x 11¾. 23587-4

THE MYTHS OF THE NORTH AMERICAN INDIANS, Lewis Spence. Rich anthology of the myths and legends of the Algonquins, Iroquois, Pawnees and Sioux, prefaced by an extensive historical and ethnological commentary. 36 illustrations. 480pp. 5⅜ x 8½. 25967-6

AN ENCYCLOPEDIA OF BATTLES: Accounts of Over 1,560 Battles from 1479 B.C. to the Present, David Eggenberger. Essential details of every major battle in recorded history from the first battle of Megiddo in 1479 B.C. to Grenada in 1984. List of Battle Maps. New Appendix covering the years 1967-1984. Index. 99 illustrations. 544pp. 6½ x 9¼. 24913-1

SAILING ALONE AROUND THE WORLD, Captain Joshua Slocum. First man to sail around the world, alone, in small boat. One of great feats of seamanship told in delightful manner. 67 illustrations. 294pp. 5⅜ x 8½. 20326-3

ANARCHISM AND OTHER ESSAYS, Emma Goldman. Powerful, penetrating, prophetic essays on direct action, role of minorities, prison reform, puritan hypocrisy, violence, etc. 271pp. 5⅜ x 8½. 22484-8

MYTHS OF THE HINDUS AND BUDDHISTS, Ananda K. Coomaraswamy and Sister Nivedita. Great stories of the epics; deeds of Krishna, Shiva, taken from puranas, Vedas, folk tales; etc. 32 illustrations. 400pp. 5⅜ x 8½. 21759-0

THE TRAUMA OF BIRTH, Otto Rank. Rank's controversial thesis that anxiety neurosis is caused by profound psychological trauma which occurs at birth. 256pp. 5⅜ x 8½. 27974-X

A THEOLOGICO-POLITICAL TREATISE, Benedict Spinoza. Also contains unfinished Political Treatise. Great classic on religious liberty, theory of government on common consent. R. Elwes translation. Total of 421pp. 5⅜ x 8½. 20249-4

CATALOG OF DOVER BOOKS

THE STORY OF THE TITANIC AS TOLD BY ITS SURVIVORS, Jack Winocour (ed.). What it was really like. Panic, despair, shocking inefficiency, and a little heroism. More thrilling than any fictional account. 26 illustrations. 320pp. 5⅜ x 8½.
20610-6

FAIRY AND FOLK TALES OF THE IRISH PEASANTRY, William Butler Yeats (ed.). Treasury of 64 tales from the twilight world of Celtic myth and legend: "The Soul Cages," "The Kildare Pooka," "King O'Toole and his Goose," many more. Introduction and Notes by W. B. Yeats. 352pp. 5⅜ x 8½.
26941-8

BUDDHIST MAHAYANA TEXTS, E. B. Cowell and others (eds.). Superb, accurate translations of basic documents in Mahayana Buddhism, highly important in history of religions. The Buddha-karita of Asvaghosha, Larger Sukhavativyuha, more. 448pp. 5⅜ x 8½.
25552-2

ONE TWO THREE . . . INFINITY: Facts and Speculations of Science, George Gamow. Great physicist's fascinating, readable overview of contemporary science: number theory, relativity, fourth dimension, entropy, genes, atomic structure, much more. 128 illustrations. Index. 352pp. 5⅜ x 8½.
25664-2

EXPERIMENTATION AND MEASUREMENT, W. J. Youden. Introductory manual explains laws of measurement in simple terms and offers tips for achieving accuracy and minimizing errors. Mathematics of measurement, use of instruments, experimenting with machines. 1994 edition. Foreword. Preface. Introduction. Epilogue. Selected Readings. Glossary. Index. Tables and figures. 128pp. 5⅜ x 8½.   40451-X

DALÍ ON MODERN ART: The Cuckolds of Antiquated Modern Art, Salvador Dalí. Influential painter skewers modern art and its practitioners. Outrageous evaluations of Picasso, Cézanne, Turner, more. 15 renderings of paintings discussed. 44 calligraphic decorations by Dalí. 96pp. 5⅜ x 8½. (Available in U.S. only.)   29220-7

ANTIQUE PLAYING CARDS: A Pictorial History, Henry René D'Allemagne. Over 900 elaborate, decorative images from rare playing cards (14th–20th centuries): Bacchus, death, dancing dogs, hunting scenes, royal coats of arms, players cheating, much more. 96pp. 9¼ x 12¼.
29265-7

MAKING FURNITURE MASTERPIECES: 30 Projects with Measured Drawings, Franklin H. Gottshall. Step-by-step instructions, illustrations for constructing handsome, useful pieces, among them a Sheraton desk, Chippendale chair, Spanish desk, Queen Anne table and a William and Mary dressing mirror. 224pp. 8⅛ x 11¼.
29338-6

THE FOSSIL BOOK: A Record of Prehistoric Life, Patricia V. Rich et al. Profusely illustrated definitive guide covers everything from single-celled organisms and dinosaurs to birds and mammals and the interplay between climate and man. Over 1,500 illustrations. 760pp. 7½ x 10⅛.
29371-8